SPEAK

Speak

SHERAE SUTTON

TyneBell Publishing

Contents

Chapter 1

The Yo- Yo Effect

I am the youngest, the shy & quiet kid "Monique. My mother didn't care for my name that much, my Father called me Mo-mo. My mother "Tommy" & father Carl Sr. had three children together including myself by the time they were nineteen & twenty. My oldest brother Carl and I really didn't have much of a relationship because we grew up in different households over the years. When I was about four I remember him living with my Grandmother Lynn, she's my father's mother. My Dad called him BJ and I couldn't understand why since his name started with a C. Shawnta, my oldest sister, is two years older than me. We called her Smiley since that's all she ever did. I have four other siblings from my dad he had with four other women. My older sister Tink, older brother Curt, my sister Dannie and lastly my youngest brother Clark. The boys thought he was gay since he had hair down his back and he cried a lot.

My Dad made sure we all knew one another despite how all our mothers felt. He said it was his duty to make sure we stayed close and stuck together at all times cause all we had in the end would be each other. Daddy would say "All I want is for all my kids to stay together." Guess things didn't turn out the way he wanted them too. Me & Shawnta were like glue, never without one another.

My mom left my dad before I was born. She said my dad was a ladies man so there was always another woman somewhere. It was just us three, Myself, my mom and my sister. People always thought my mom was our sister because of how young she looked. My mother's mother, grandmother Dawn, was in and out of our lives. One minute she was there then I wouldn't see her for a while. Along with the in and out of my Grandma Dawn my Grandpa Monty added another interesting chapter to our family story. My Grandpa had his wife Kim, whom we called "Lil Bit" because of her height. She was pretty young when I met her. My Grandpa had one kid with her, My Aunt Megan. Me and Aunt Megan were three years apart so we grew up more like sisters. Then on the other hand my grandfather and grandma Dawn had four children together. My mother Tommy, Uncle Ronald, Uncle Luke, who grandma Dawn used to call him Sugarman, & Uncle Rick.

We stayed upstairs in a family flat with our cousin KK, one of my Grandma Dawn's nieces. Grandpa and Grandma Lil-bit were pregnant with Megan & Grandma Dawn stayed downstairs in the same house. Trust me I have to laugh now just thinking about how crazy this shit sounds. They made it work. Honestly, it was hard to believe they could be in the same room let alone under the same roof.

My mom and all of my Aunts and Uncles grew up in the system due to my grandma Dawn having a mental illness and also being on drugs. Grandpa Monty was a big time drug dealer back in the day as well. So between one parent being on drugs and the other in the streets my mother pretty much played the mom to Uncle Ron & Sugarman. Mom went from living house to house with family to foster homes & girl homes until she couldn't take anymore of the bouncing around. At this point she had my oldest brother Carl and she left the last foster home she stayed in because the foster parents were abusing Carl. Grandma Lynn took her and Carl in and not long after she got pregnant with Shawnta. Uncle Ron went his way and got into the game with my grandpa, Sugarman went back into the system, and Uncle Rick was a baby, he got adopted by a family from Houston, Texas. Word around the family, someone slipped grandma a "mickey" and she was never the same, she turned to drugs. It's fucked up how rough they had it coming up, just couldn't understand how a mother could be so self-ish to let drugs destroy everything. There's nothing like a mother's love, right? Well how would you know if you never received it? I always wondered what that felt like to have that motherly love, guess you can't give what you never had. Once I understood the dynamics that my mother grew up in it helped me see how the course of my life was set long before I was born. I'm coming to understand a lot of the things I may have faulted her for were out of her control. She was dealt a hand and she was just playing with the cards she was dealt.

A lot of people say it's impossible to remember cer-tain things if you are too young. I'm here to tell you that's a damn lie. I was small enough to remember climb-ing in and out of one of those play-pins. I remember how much I hated that family flat house we lived in. I was young but the amount of roaches that were in that house a person can never forget, they were everywhere. I remember seeing some of my cousins throwing a black leather couch we had in the front room off the top of the balcony because of all the roaches. Yes, I remember us moving out with all of our stuff in black trash bags. I don't know why maybe the roaches ran us away. Mom found a house on the west side of Detroit on a blocked name Spokane right across from an elementary school. It was a nice big house black and white on the outside and huge on the inside. Big front room with gray carpet, dining room with momma's room to the left of it. The bathroom in the middle to separate me & Shawnta's room. The kitchen was set up like a bar. It had the already built in stools, plush seats with a room right across from it. We loved that house and it was one of the first houses I actually can say I grew up in for a few years. It was the four of us this time, Carl, Shawnta, me and mom. She did everything she could. She was so young with three kids. Between working and them two in school I had to be watched since I was too young to start school, her hands were full. My birthday was late which kept me from starting school. So I spent a lot of time with Aunt Megan & Grandma Lil-bit when mommy had to work. Life was good & fun around that time. She made sure we were good and comfortable and she did her best to keep us happy.

Funniest moment was when mommy and all of us were running from the little mouse that got into the house one winter. She chased the mouse down in the kitchen with the broom and all of us were running around screaming. Every time the ice cream truck came Carl & Shawnta would run outside the door while I stood at the screen with mommy she would yell "make sure y'all get Mo-Mo one too"! Moments like that I can't ever forget. These were the moments that gave me a little hope that the future was much more than the roach infested craziness I felt like I was becoming comfortable with. I knew that there could be better because my mom had put us in a position to experience better.

Carl was diagnosed with ADHD before I was born. It was a whole story about how my mom tried to kill Carl with a bottle of iron pills & how he was supposed to die on his first birthday because she found out about my dad dating someone else. Nobody will ever know the true story cause nobody was there. However, he was very active & hyper all the time. One time he saw the ice cream truck and he ran right through the screen door, busting his head open. He ended up with a scarf for life. Till this day thinking about that makes me laugh, the boy had no chill. I remember momma putting Carl in the tub cause he had an allergic reaction to something or caught ringworm from outside. The neighbor told mom to put bleach in his bath water to stop the itching. That was the worst thing that could have been done. Mom called Grandma Lynn and she came & got Carl, had him for a whole week & never brought him back home. Grandma Lynn lied and made up this big story that child protective services had been out to her house & was supposed to make a trip to our house as well. She threatened to take me & Shawnta if mom didn't sign Carl over to her. Momma was young & didn't know any better. It crushed my mom, hurt her soul. She never got him back after that. Grandma Dawn had to come live with us because mom picked up more hours at work to get money for a lawyer. She needed a full time sitter. She was in & out of court a lot fighting to get Carl back. Grandma Dawn had to be our babysitter for a while. Me & Shawnta loved toys. We had no choice but to play together since we barely could watch TV anymore. Grandma Dawn would be tripping, always turning the channel or putting damn towels over the screen saying people were talking to her through the TV. Shit was irritating the hell outta us. She barely could even cook food for us because she would burn everything so momma didn't want her in the kitchen. My grandma was the only person I know that made a meal in the dark.

When Uncle Luke turned seventeen he came to stay with us because his foster mother needed help with him. I think her name was Mrs. Murphy. They made some type of agreement that my mom would help her out since she was getting too old. Uncle Luke would be going back & forth with us and her house. I just don't get why she felt the need to take on much more responsibilities since we were enough. Uncle Luke didn't talk much. He stayed to himself in the extra room in the back by the kitchen. We thought something was wrong with him. He would isolate himself in the room all the time.

Around this time Momma met this guy named Tony, a light-skinned tall guy with a bald head. He took mom out a lot, a really nice guy. When mommy introduced him he walked up to us & said,

"Hey Shawnta & Monique it's finally nice to meet y'all, y'all being good listening to your mother?"

We responded "yes" laughing.

He told us he had kids too. He asked us if it was ok to take momma & us out on a movie date. From that moment mommy and Tony were kicking it hard. He would take us places to his moms house, movies, buy us whatever we wanted, toys and stuff for Christmas, and take us for rides in his car. That song "They Don't Know About Us" by Tony B he said that's how he felt about my mom. Man, we really liked that man. He showed he cared for all of us. Hell daddy wasn't in the picture at this time, so he played like a daddy role. He asked us one day when he was over with his two sons, did we want him and my mommy to be together and all of us were on the living room floor yelling "YES"!

Don't know what happened months down the line but we stopped seeing Tony as much. Guess some shit just doesn't work out. Really don't think my mom liked him as much as he liked her. It was back to the basics just us again. It was a Sunday when Megan spent the night and nobody came to pick her back up. We were both at the house with my grandma watching us. We were running around from room to room since we were the only ones that weren't in school. We had to play in the house. Grandma Dawn was watching a blank TV laughing talking to herself, so we ran into Uncle Luke's room and started messing with his stuff. He had a turtle and game system he rigged to work. However, we weren't supposed to be messing with plugs but we put it in the wall anyway. The TV didn't work so we went back out in the front with grandma Dawn and started playing around the TV. Before I knew it we smelt smoke, looked up and saw black smoke flowing across the ceiling from the back room.

Megan yelled "Dawn! it's smoking in the back"!

She got up and said "the house is on fire" But she just stood there!

Both of us grabbed her hands and ran out the front door. The fire spread so fast the house looked like it was almost in flames. Momma pulled up out of nowhere screaming "Not my house!" "NO!!" The window from Luke's room blew out and glass shattered from the side of the house. Flames covered the side of the house. All I could see was mommy face covered in tears. I watched her cry so hard I began to cry. The only words that left her mouth was "My house!!!" "What happened?"

"Where are we going to go now?" momma said.

Giving me a hug while Megan was covered in black smoke. All she had on was her underwear and a long white shirt with her curly hair to her butt with no shoes. I was still in pajamas as well. We were able to tell what happened. This big white guy that had on a huge yellow and red suit put us in the fire truck to check us out. He began to ask us what happened so we told him. Once he left out the truck I started laughing. I just couldn't stop looking at Megan and all the black smoke she had on her face. Megan was extremely light. She could go for a white girl so you just imagine seeing a white girl covered in some black smoke lmao...

Megan started cracking up, looked at me and said, " yo dumb ass telling everything nigga, you the one who started the fire."

I laughed and said, "No Carrie white you started it", then we both said "nigga we both did it, shut up!"

Even with the laughter, it still was a sad day for everyone because I knew everything my mom went through to get us somewhere comfortable & stable. That was our home we watched go up in flames. Even though it was a mistake, it still was hurtful to my mother. So of course we had to find somewhere else to go.

Momma had a guy friend we met who went by the name Cain. A tall dark brown skinned man had a gold tooth with a jerry curl. He reminded me of a pimp. We moved into one of his properties. He owned a big four story hotel on the westside of Detroit off of Livernois and Joy road behind the railroad tracks. I'm not sure if he owned it or if he was doing business out of it but It was super big and had so many rooms. We stayed in the basement. It was finished and we had a bedroom set that all three of us slept in. Carl still wasn't with us. He was still with grandma Lynn and Carl every time something happened with my mom she would use that as ammo for why Carl shouldnt be back with us. It was as if she took these opportunities just to be devilish. Kicking my mom when she was already down, knowing that her son was one of her weak points.

It was the next day and mommy needed to run some errands, so Cain took her. This particular day he and mommy went to the store. Felt like they were only gone for fifteen minutes and told us to stay outside in the front to ride our bikes. He said the clerks at the front desk & one of his female housekeepers would keep an eye on us until they got back. We started running around outside. It was a railroad track they didn't want us playing by. We ran after each other into the hotel. There were so many rooms, some people were in them, some were empty with the TV playing porn. I went into one of the rooms into the bathroom to hide in the tub.

I heard Shawnta calling out for me yelling, "we have to go back outside they're back."

I came out of the bathroom and saw a man on top of a woman naked playing on the TV. My eyes blew up and I started watching it for a second.This was my first time seeing people having sex. That was the first time I felt a tingling sensation in my vagina. I feel like my innocence at this moment was gone. I was exposed to something that I had never seen before and my body had a reaction that I truly didn't understand. The statement I use to hear all the time is "watch what you do & say around your kids." Now I know for myself the true understanding of this statement because I was forever changed after that day.

Shawnta ran past the room yelling again "Come on Mo-Mo they're here". Cain had told us we weren't supposed to be in the rooms so she was trying to keep me from getting in trouble. I went back into the hallway and closed the door,

"What were you doing?" "Where were you?" Shawnta said.

She couldn't find me. I said "Did you see that stuff playing on the TV?" She grabbed my hand and we ran back downstairs. They had just got out of the car walking towards the entrance doors as we were walking out mom asked,

"Where was y'all at?" Both of us replied "we had to use the bathroom."

Cain handed us a bag of junk food and we looked at each other and started smiling and said "Thank you." Cain was a cool cat as they called those types of guys. They called them sugar daddies. He was way older than mommy; she was only in her twenties. I knew him and momma messed around as much as they called themselves trying to hide it. He did a lot of stuff for her and us, hell, I started to think he was our daddy. Those kinds of men had wives hidden somewhere along with tons of women and kids. He even let Grandma Dawn come stay with us as well. The basement was getting small even though we didn't stay there that long. Cain took mommy to look for a house on the eastside. Surprisingly she found us a house way off of State Fair and 75 Freeway on Cameron Street. Seemed anywhere we've stayed had schools all around.

Another big white house with a concrete long porch with black banisters all around, nice size backyard with a garage and a long driveway with a silver gate. The dark brown wooden floors from the shining living room and dining room were so clean they were combined together which made it look giant. Two bedrooms on the main floor. Which was going to be moms and grandma Dawn bedrooms. My mom's bathroom was really small and had a little window high from the ground off the driveway. Then there was the biggest room in the house. The upstairs had a flight of brown cracky stairs with a ledge that was like four rooms in one. It had four closets, one side would be Shawnta and I would have a whole side. We were so excited about how huge our room was shit because it felt like we had our own space. The basement was the last place we looked, so we went through the kitchen. It was an old brown wood door with a rusted door handle. It was full of darkness when I opened the door and looked down. The steps were steep and very spaced apart. Only light you could see was from the kitchen's light. Momma flicked a switch and it turned on a light. "Now we can go down and see," Momma said. There was no handle to hold onto to walk down. You had to walk down, touching the wall or you could easily fall to the basement floor. I could see the red peeled paint on the walls as we walked down the stairs. It was cold with concrete flooring so it wasn't a finished basement. I can see why it was so dark there were two little windows from the backyard. There was a big space to the right of the stairs and there was a big hand built wooden room. I don't know if it was supposed to be a storage room or not, however, there was a white string hanging from the tall ceiling for the light. The room looked very creepy and gave me the chills. Never would've thought this room would be part of my worst nightmare and forever change my life.

The day we were supposed to move in the landlord had to do a few touch ups before we moved our things in. He gave her an extra day to still get the little things together plus Grandma Dawn stuff that was left at the hotel. Next day we all were pretty excited to move and we couldn't stop talking about our room. It was feeling good outside, good weather and sunshine makes you happy. Cain had brought momma a brand new car, a blue two door Cavalier she was so happy! Brand new car and house we were set! Everything he did for her he must have really loved my momma and he helped us move everything in afterwards. He made sure she or we didn't need anything before he left and gave us a hug. All you saw was that gold tooth shining from the front of his mouth smiling telling us goodbye and to keep in touch. We didn't see as much of Cain after.

However, there was this one guy named Mario that we saw around for a moment. He was cocky, dark skinned with a bald head. In a white old school car with tints on his windows. There wasn't anything I liked about him. He gave off a bad vibe and I just felt he was up to no good. This one morning I heard lots of bumping downstairs. I asked Shawnta if she heard it as well. We started hearing screams right after. The both of us got up and ran down. The screams were coming from mama's room.

"Get off of me, let me go now!" "Shut up bitch, lay down," he said.

She screamed and screamed for us to help her. I ran to the kitchen yelling for Uncle Luke to come upstairs. As he was walking up Shawnta and I loudly said "You don't hear our mama in the room yelling?"

"I don't have anything to do with that, it's not my business," he said.

Shawnta said "That's your sister, how could you not help her? He's in there hurting her!"

"I'm not getting in her mess, that's her business!" He yelled again. I started crying because hearing my mom call for help and being a kid I couldn't do anything. I ran to her door and banged on it screaming "Get off my mama!"

Shawnta stood at the room door. "Come on Mo let's just go upstairs." I kept turning on her doorknob trying to get it open, but it was locked. "Get off Mario," she yelled again. He opened the door then ran out. Holding his pants up with his left hand. He didn't have on a shirt nor shoes. I went in there quickly and Shawnta followed. Mama was laid on her stomach across her bed completely naked. Both of her hands were tied up with my brown belt with colorful stones in it. He also took her string from her flower robe and tied it around her mouth.

"Are you okay mama?" I asked "Hurry up and get me loose." she replied in a voice that felt so feeling less.

We got her loose fast. She threw on her robe and ran outside. He was still in the driveway trying to get his car started. She had his shoes in her hand and began banging on his driver window.

"You mother fucking rapist she screamed out! You tied me up bitch I'm calling the police.", She screamed loudly.

His car finally started. Quickly pulling out the driveway and driving off. He rode down his window and put his middle finger up laughing at her. We were standing on the porch. "Go in the house now," she said. Running back in grabbing the phone. She called him, cursing him out. She slammed the phone down on the dining table.

She looked up and saw us looking at her and said, "I'm okay y'all go back upstairs." I was hurt seeing my mom tied up like that. I was glad he never came back around.

Chapter 2

Let's Come Together

It was the summer of 1995 we were driving down the block in the uphaul truck Cameron Street was full of kids playing everywhere. Our first summer on the new block, I was happy to see as many kids since I didn't have any friends. There were kids out from each corner running around riding their bikes and more. As we pulled into the driveway and got out the truck to go into the house a few girls rode past on their bikes and spoke to us. We waved back and went into the house. The sun was shining right through the windows. There were no blinds or shades up yet. Mom yelled out, let's get started while it's still early. We didn't have too much stuff to get off the truck besides our clothes and toys and the new beds. We had to start over after the house caught fire. Soon after we were done we asked to go outside on the porch. We saw three girls next door who were outside playing with chalk. They looked like they were sisters. An older lady to the left of us sitting in her black chair on the porch smoking a cigarette.

The girl's mom came outside and yelled out "Hi, how y'all doing?"

She had the funniest, loudest voice like a baby almost like her voice never matured with her age. My mom came out and both introduced themselves to each other. The girls from down the street rode their bikes back to us and asked our names and asked,

"This y'all new house now?" "Yes" we replied "we just moved all our stuff in. I'm Shawnta and my sister Mo-mo." My sister introduced us.

Shawnta and I actually fit right in with all the girls on the block. All of us were either the same age or close in age with each other. We got pretty close with the girls next door Donna, Danyell, and Dream. She was the youngest and later became my best friend & their little sister Diamond was born a year later. Their mom Debra was a very cool and nice momma and she became good friends. The kids who were two houses down from Miss. Debra were the kids we called full house kids Layla and all of her brothers and sisters she had to look after since her mom was barely ever home. When their mom was home she beat them so loud you would hear them screaming from outside. It would be days before they came back out until the bruises went away. The teenage boy Q at the end of the block all the girls thought he was drop dead gorgeous tall brown-skinned with a nice smile plus he played basketball. He reminded me so much of Q in the movie Love & Basketball. He and Donna started going together and it wasn't a surprise they were the same age. Next to Q was Sally, the only kid at the end of the block by herself. Sally was a complete spoiled brat that cried about everything. Only time she was extremely happy was when she was in the boys' faces. Showing off her long hair and big tits. She was practically raised by her 70 year old grandmother that beat the hell out of her with switches from the backyard for acting grown. She could never leave in front of her house. Her mom was never really there and spent most of her time chasing guys Momma said she was following in her mom's footsteps very young. Momma didn't care too much for me playing with her, but she still let me sometimes. Sally's Aunt Joy stayed next door to us. Mrs. Joy was always in her black chair smoking a cigarette & her teenage granddaughter Tina stayed with her. She was one of the sweetest women you could ever meet. She couldn't stand the kids who stayed next to her cause they had roaches. She told momma them damn things go house to house if you had them really bad which they did.

One day I knocked at their door to see if they could come outside to play. There were roaches crawling on the outside of their door. It became a habit to knock and run down so that I wouldn't be too close to the door when they opened the door. I was never allowed to go inside their house, momma said. Bella, the girl who had a slight disability, was so pretty & only could ride her bike when the sun came down and most of the kids went into the house. She had an older mom and I was the only one her mom would let her play with. The bad ghetto kids with the crazy mom Pauline. It was five of them Mike, Sherry, Marty, Chrissy, & Drea, always fighting or in trouble but we got along for the most part until somebody got mad you know how kids stuff goes. Can't forget about Felicia & James. They were the last house off the corner of the block next to the abortion clinic with the berry tree in front of it. Everyone of us ate the berries from that tree. They were raised by their grandparents Felicia the oldest. James was a terrible kid out of control and disrespectful to their grandparents. He irritated the hell out of all of us at times.

One day he took a shit on the side of our house cause he didn't feel like running home. Just because he wanted to finish playing freeze tag with everybody. Everyone got pretty close and all of the parents got to know each other. Everyone on the block was like family after a while. Being in one of the last generations that grew up on blocks like this made me realize how important having other kids and families to be around growing up is. Neighborhoods with a lot of kids and different family dynamics are where some of the greatest kids come from. Those village type streets, rather good or bad, are stitched in my memory of growing up. Building those relationships allowed us to sleepovers at each other's houses whenever it was one of our birthdays. Everyone came together and went bike riding and walked to the corner stores. There was a Catholic church mixed with a special education school where we went across the street to play. We called it the square. A few of us would go over there inside the school to help serve the disabled kids in wheelchairs and push them around to their tables to eat lunch. They would give us free snacks and juices for helping out. It was a big field that was gated off that we could run around and play in after all the kids were loaded on the buses to be taken home.

Playing all of those fun kid games like, "zing zing zing like a washing machine" or slide the hand game, "Mr. Fox what time is it" and of course "Mrs. Mary Mack." I could go on & on. We even would have little sing offs.

These singing battles are when I discovered my voice. I honestly didn't even know my ass knew how to sing! Yep, I could blow when I wanted, and for the first time actually letting everybody on the block hear me. I got so tired of Sally ass always trying to out sing everybody even though she did have a nice voice. One day we were across the street singing behind the church. Sally snuck down the street to Mrs. Joy house and she let her go across the street with us. I started blowing & blew her ass out the park.

"Damn, who can sing in your family? How did you get a voice like that?" Drea asked.

"I want to become a singer when I grow up. I don't know where I got it from but I have big dreams." I said. What made it even better is I believed in everything I dreamed of to be so young.

The summer was coming to an end and mom had to get us registered and ready for one of the schools in the neighborhood. She decided to enroll us in the school John C. Marshall that was a few blocks down the street from the house. We could walk home with all our friends when she couldn't pick us up from school. Momma let Uncle Luke come stay with us again before school started. We needed a babysitter for when she went to work in the morning. She let him move downstairs in the basement. He made the creepy storage room his bedroom and fixed it up and everything. He started giving me big bags of Tootsie Frooties he got from the corner store. That's why grandma Dawn gave him the name Sugarman, he was tall 6 '3 light skinned and had braces. He still gave off a weird vibe since he didn't talk to us much at the other house. All he used to do was sit in the room playing his game. This time he was in the basement a lot watching TV or he would sit downstairs in the bed whenever I went down there to get the clothes from the dryer. Shawnta & I were kind of bothered for a minute just felt like we wanted to finally have our house to ourselves for once just us and momma. Of course it didn't matter what we wanted, we had no choice. Momma said he was only staying with us for a little while, nevertheless, that little while turned into four years. People would've thought Uncle Luke was our brother at some point, shit, mommy played the role of his mother anyway.

Three weeks before school started momma started her new job. It wasn't that bad at first until hours went by and I started to cry for her. I clinged very close to her so I didn't like when she would be gone for too long. To keep me from crying Uncle Luke would let us go outside. It was hot outside so he sat on the porch & watched us play with everybody. Debra would let us come over in front of her house whenever Donna was on the porch looking after Danyell and Dream. After so many times of us being at home with Uncle Luke, Debra would just tell me and Shawnta to come over.

She would say, "little girls shouldn't be at home with a man all day." "I don't care if he's family or not."

Whenever she would take the girls out to carnivals and stuff she'd tell us to call and ask momma or tell Luke to tell momma we were going with them. At that time I never understood what she meant by us not always being home with Uncle Luke, because he was our family and what could he possibly do to one of us. The summer had come to an end. It was time for everybody to go back to school. I was starting kindergarten and Shawnta was in second grade. I was super nervous being around a lot of kids I didn't know; so I peed on myself for a while. Momma would have to pack me an extra change of clothes or come get me from school for the first few weeks. I got over that in due time because I started making friends. I started loosening up and liking school. I made a friend named Arie. We were the same age and our birthdays were a week apart. She started calling me her best friend. I was cool with her calling me her best friend because she was my first friend at the school. Then I met Kya. She was the biggest crybaby even though she irritated everybody it was like the few of us kind of stuck together. When school would let out me, Shawnta, Arie and her sisters would walk home together since they stayed a few blocks across the bridge from us.

Uncle Luke met us at the corner or in front of the church the days momma was at work and couldn't pick us up. She would tell him to make us sandwiches, pizza rolls, chicken nuggets, or fish sticks until she made it home. Sometimes momma didn't want us outside until she got home and made sure we did our homework. She didn't like all the kids in front of our house or on the porch when she got home. She would get super annoyed by that. Uncle Luke would tell us after we finished eating we had to do homework after then we could play with our toys or watch TV.

Grandma Dawn was always gone around the corner at her guy friend's Timothy house or at the drug house two blocks over. Grandma Dawn and Luke didn't get along. He would yell at her or be mean to her at times. That's why she stayed gone most of the time. My Mom didn't get off until five-thirty some days, so we would sit up on the game system until mommy got us. When we got bored Uncle Luke would scare us into playing tag running around the house screaming. One time we were playing he grabbed a knife and chased us around the house then fell on the floor and pretended to be dead. Anybody would've thought he was dead! Only time he would stop is when we both said we didn't want to play any more. After school one day Uncle Luke let us go outside to play. I went down to Sally's house while Shawnta rode her bike back and forth down the street. She was going fast while Marty was chasing her around and pushed Shawnta off her bike.

I heard her crying from Sally's house yelling "I'm going to get my Uncle" and Marty yelling "I don't care go get him."

I ran as fast as I could back home.

She was crying to Uncle Luke, he came outside on the porch yelling "Who pushed her off her bike?" Marty said "I did but we were just playing." No you didn't, he did it on purpose!

I don't know why Chrissy and Drea came running in front of our house talking junk. Of course I stood up for my sister and told them to get their dirty asses from in front of our house! That was the first time I ever cussed in front of anybody.

Luke told Marty "You are a boy and these are little girls. Why are you even playing with them? Aren't you way older than them? Don't be putting your hands on my niece then go on and tell the girls don't come back down to our house since y'all talking junk!"

Dirty asses got mad and said they were going to get Mike crazy ass. Uncle Luke yelled out "I DON'T CARE GO GET HIM!"

Shit that was the dumbest thing his ass could've ever said and momma wasn't there. Uncle Luke walked to the store later on that day when the sun went down once momma made it home. Me and Shawnta were sitting in the front room watching TV when momma asked one of us to get up and close the door.

We heard screaming "OPEN THE DOOR!" "Momma you hear that?" Shawnta got up to look. It's Luke yelling momma.

As we got up it was Luke running up on the porch and Mike black ass chasing after him. My heart was racing; it was like a tall circus clown running for dear life! Luke fell onto the stairs. Mike grabbed one of his shoes causing him to hit the porch hard. They both swung but missed.

Mike yelling out, "what's all that shit you were talking about earlier?"

Marty lying ass told him that Luke had been cursing at him and pushed him off the porch.

"That's a lie he never did," said Shawnta. Momma ran outside like a gangsta and pushed Mike off Luke.

She shouted "Nigga get the fuck off my brother! Luke get the fuck up nigga you don't run from no fucking body. Now if you wanna fight do it now!" "Nah, Tommy I'm not about to fight this man. For what?" "Yeah, whatever nigga just say you scared." Momma yelled, "Ain't nobody scared of your dirty ass get the fuck off my porch and from in front of my crib. Luke, get the hell in the house." "Why are you sticking up for his grown ass?" asked Marty. "Little kid because that's what the fuck you are- Mike get your brother I'm not trying to hear that bullshit."

She stood on the porch as she watched them walk back down, came in then slammed the door. Momma was beyond pissed.

"What in the fuck happened earlier?" She yelled. Shawnta told her everything and that was the end of us going down to their house and playing with them. Still didn't stop us from playing with everybody else though, it didn't do anything but make me, Dream, Shawnta and Danyell even closer. They weren't allowed to play with them anyways. Donna was always ready to fight them. She said they were jealous and mad. They knew not to come down here and fuck with us. Donna was crazy and Debra didn't play. Debra and mom got so tight we began having sleepovers and birthday parties together. Momma and Debra would have card night and drink on the weekends. I remember them riding out on Diamond's dad when she was a few months old. She caught him cheating or something and my momma was right by her side with our asses in the backseat at five in the morning! A few weeks later they seemed a bit distant from one another, things seemed to be awkward and we stopped going over as much. It didn't stop us from playing with each other though.

One day Shawnta and Danyell were going back and forth about a bike and Donna said something to Shawnta that made her cry. All I know is momma came out of the house like sonic and jumped on Donna. Shit happened so fast I couldn't believe it even happened. I was more disappointed with momma because Donna wasn't grown but momma kept screaming "I'm not your momma or a fucking kid." Debra started yelling that Donna needed the butt whooping, that she wasn't breaking shit up and she needed to stay in a kids place! Uncle Luke came out and broke up the fight. She continued to hold her down on the ground pushing her head to the ground hitting her then I heard Debra say "Okay that's enough now!" This was the worst weekend ever and I was so ready to get away. It didn't matter even if it was just going to school, something needed to shake fast! There was another friendship down the drain. I just knew me and Dream friendship was over. All of the feeling of family and togetherness that we felt in the beginning of moving there was beginning to fade away. I often look back and try to figure out what played a role in the destruction of some of those relationships. I thought some of the people would be in my life forever but life had different plans.

Chapter 3

When it all Happened......

It was nice outside and we were in the house on this good Saturday. Momma let us decide if we wanted to leave or stay home. Confused on if I wanted to go over to my Dad's, grandma Lynn or grandpa Monty's house with Megan. I went wherever Shawnta wanted to go, but we decided we wanted to stay home. Megan wanted me to come over anyways. I didn't want to leave home if Shawnta didn't; I told her to ask grandma and grandpa Monty if she could come over. We were like salt and pepper inseparable. She made me promise her if she came over that I would come over the following weekend so they brought her over. On some weekends momma went out to the clubs with our older cousins and her friends. Today she was out running errands, shopping. Uncle Luke was watching us until she got back home. He and Megan didn't care for each other. I think it was because he was no longer the youngest and she was. Maybe it was a jealousy thing. He got very irritated whenever she came around. He seemed annoyed; he would say it's because she talked too much. Megan was always ready to play so we were running around upstairs making all kinds of noise. Shawnta started playing with us so Uncle Luke came to our room door telling us we were too loud. Megan yelled out, telling him to shut up and go back downstairs.

He yelled back upstairs "Who do you think you are talking to, little girl?" He ran up the stairs so fast he hit his head and stumbled backwards to the floor. He looked like he had passed out laying on the floor. One thing for sure he was a good actor. He could make you believe damn near anything. He stayed down on the hardwood floor for at least five minutes.

He pretended to be dead. Waiting for us to crowd around him which we did yelling "Luke get up!" Megan giggled and said "that nigga dead" he opened his eyes and began screaming! We all started screaming, running downstairs. He got up off that floor so fast it was like the walking dead running after us. We were running from closet to closet hiding under grandma Dawn and momma's bed. Shawnta said she was tired of playing because that kind of stuff scared her so she went back upstairs to watch tv. When Megan and I creeped from Grandma Dawn's room Luke was laid out on the front room floor on his stomach. There were some small toys left by the couch from us playing with earlier. I grabbed them and gave her a few. We creeped on our knees to him, giggling. I put my index finger up to my lips so she could stop laughing. Spit running down her bottom lip from the laughter. I had the idea to put the toys on his pants and run back to hide. That's exactly what we did when we peeked back in here. I noticed the toys were not sitting on the top of his dark blue sweatpants. His sweatpants were down and you could see the print of the toys inside of his underwear. Megan whispered in my ear "He nasty" and chuckled but I didn't think it was that funny. That meant we had to go in his underwear while he was still laid out. I told Megan I wasn't going to get them out. She insisted on grabbing it.

"You're acting like a real PUNK.", She said. "Let's both get them together since both put them there." I said.

With her hand up high counting down with her fingers 3,2,1 we pulled his drawls down to his butt cheeks. There were tons of black hairs covering his entire butt. The toys were sitting where his balls were and half of his dick tip showing. Megan giggled as we both reached and grabbed them. I whispered to her "let's just go back upstairs and play with Shawnta". "Dang, I thought y'all were done playing" said Shawnta. I'm not sure how long he laid on the floor since we were no longer down there.

It was the afternoon. We were hungry after all that running around playing. Shawnta said "Lets go downstairs to tell Luke we're hungry." So we followed her down the stairs. We made it to the kitchen. Shawnta yelled out she wasn't playing no more just in case he decided to jump out to scare us. That didn't make a difference. He came out of nowhere and screamed at the top of his lungs! I damn near peed on myself from how bad he scared all of us. I thought that shit was creepy. Why are you constantly scaring girls anyway? He saw us balled up in the corner next to the stove.

"Okay, I'll let y'all breathe for a while. I bet y'all won't bother me any more now."

"Luke, can you make us some pizza rolls and fries before you go back downstairs to your room?" Shawnta said.

"YES, I'll let y'all know when it's ready it'll be on the stove just come get it Shawnta." He told us as he turned away. Shawnta bought our food back up there on a paper plate. None of us went back downstairs until momma got back in the house. When she made it back we ran downstairs, "Hey momma, what did you get from the store?" "Nothing much, just something to wear for tonight,"She said. "Ma, can we go outside and play please? It's boring here." We said hoping she would free us from the house. "Don't take y'all asses anywhere down this street. Better yet, ride your bike on the other side of the street. I don't want to whoop nobody's ass today." She said, We did just what she said and played at the square with each other for a few hours until she called us back into the house. "Girls, it's time!" That meant bring your ass in the house now. "I'm about to get dinner ready while y'all take turns bathing." She said,

I didn't know how to wash myself up properly for a long time. Mama did that shit until I was at least seven. "Y'all been playing in pajamas all day. Mo-mo and Megan you two can take a bath together to save some hot water for Shawnta to shower." Megan hated brushing her teeth and washing up. She instantly got upset saying she was ready to go home. "Oh yeah, no. You're about to call daddy and Lil Bit to come pick your ass up. I'm not dealing with the nasty shit today!" My mama said as she walked over to get the phone. The phone was on speaker when Grandma Lil Bit answered the phone. I could hear Megan crying telling her she was ready to come home! "Why Megan?" Grandma Lil Bit asked, with momma yelling in the back-round saying "She over here being nasty as always Lil Bit!" Grandma screamed through the phone "Wash up!" Megan yelled back, "Come get me." Dang, yeah, she was disrespectful but it wasn't even her fault there was no control or respect because grandpa Monty was in the streets and grandma was a user. Eating junk and running around outside was her life. She did what-ever she wanted. Being around us was her only time to be a normal kid. Although she was a bit much at her age I was glad when she came around because she stopped a lot from happening some days.

Once grandpa Monty came and got her there was nothing for me to do. Shawnta didn't want to play all the time. Her eyes were stuck to the television for the day. Dinner was ready. Momma whipped up a fast meal of fried chicken, peas, and mac and cheese. I could smell it from upstairs. My stomach was growling. After I got my clothes on from bathing I ran down to the kitchen and sat at the table. Watching momma take the last of the chicken out of the grease, laying it on the paper towel. "Alright Shawnta and Luke the food is done come get your plates," mama said. Luke standing at the basement door with Shawnta sitting next to me. She placed our plates in front of us. Strongly she said, "Make sure y'all eat all of it cause I'm not making anything else." Handing Luke his plate "Yeah, nigga, you need a job it's not a lot of food. You know I have to feed them first." "Thanks sis, I know I appreciate you for letting me stay here though." he said Then went back down to his room.

"Well I'm about to get ready so I can head out soon. I'm not trying to be out all night." She said. "Mama, can we have some hot sauce on our chicken?" We asked. Frown on her face, "I'll pour it because Shawnta just overdo it." She made the best fried chicken and we smashed our food within minutes. Throwing my chicken bones into the trash Luke came up to throw his stuff away meeting me at the garbage. He stared me in my eyes with a smirk on his face. I smiled back and he walked over to the sink putting our plates in here. I went into the front room after washing my hands and sat on the couch and began watching America's Funniest Videos. "Shawnta that funny show on again, come watch it with me."I yelled. Mama screamed from the bathroom. "Mo-mo bring me my towel." I got up from the couch to grab it from her room but, before I could, I saw Luke sitting at the table like he was waiting for something.

"Here mama." "Thank you, baby."

"Mama, are you coming back home tonight?" "Yes, I'll be back shortly."

Whenever she said that I just knew that wasn't true. "I need a breath of fresh air," she said. Grandma Dawn came walking in through the front door just in time. With excitement in my voice, "Are you staying here with us?" I asked. When Uncle Luke saw her he rolled his eyes with irritation and went downstairs. "Mo-mo, nope. I'm getting ready to head back out to my friend's house a few blocks up."

I pouted with my arms crossed flopping back down to the couch. I was my grandma's favorite and I loved her no matter how many drugs she did. Perfume filled the air from mama's room with heels clacking to the wood floors. "I'm about to head out. LUKE, come here," mama said. "Don't keep your ass down in that basement all night playing the game leaving my kids to watch themselves. Look after the girls please. I won't be gone too long, page me or call me on my cell if you need anything. Mo-mo give me a hug. Don't cry I'll be back. Call me before y'all go to sleep," then out the door she went. Luke sat at the dining table across from the couch. "What's wrong with you?" he asked me. "I didn't want my mama to leave." "Oh she'll be back, you're getting too big for that!" Grandma Dawn coming out of the bathroom yelling Shawnta's name "You alright up there?" She replied "Yes grandma, I'm okay just watching tv." "Okay, I'll see y'all later." Mo-mo dragging her feet walking to the door "Be good." "I'm locking the door so if you don't have your key you won't get back in," Luke shouted. She ignored him and continued to walk out the door. "I have some candy and chips downstairs for y'all you want some?" Luke asked. "Yes, I do," I replied quietly. "Come on so you can give Shawnta some too."

He grabbed my hand and guided me down slowly. I couldn't understand why it was so dark. "Where's the light Uncle Luke? I can't see anything." I said as I walked down the stairs. My feet were cold from touching the basement floor without socks on. We stopped and he reached for the string to turn the light on. He sat me on the bed and began looking on both sides of his bed for the snacks "Oh here it is. I thought I ate it all," chuckling. "Thank you." I said, "I'm about to go give Shawnta some." Almost fifty pieces of candy were in a sandwich bag so I split it and gave Shawnta a bag of chips. "Where you get this from?" She asked. "Uncle Luke gave it to me and said we can have it,"I said, smiling ear to ear. "Oh that's my favorite movie-Ant Life. I want to watch it with you."I said, and sat on the bean bag while she laid on her bed. Laughing, eating our snacks, "That's a crazy ant!" laughing loudly. Creaks from the stairs from Uncle Luke creeping up slowly. Shaentae noticed him staring from the stairs. He peeked his head over the banister saying "Just checking to see if y'all ok. Mo, did you share your snacks with Tae?" "Yes she gave me some, thank you," Shawnta said.

"Mo-mo when you're done come here." I didn't know what he wanted but I got right up after he went down. "Yes, Uncle Luke?" I yelled out. Then he called for me again. "Yeah I'm down here."

He had made it to the basement. I walked down to his room and he was laid back on his bed with his arms behind his head. The tv playing commercials "You can come sit on the bed if you want. What do you want to watch?" He asked. "We were watching Ant's up there." I said. Handing me his remote, "Put whatever you want on," then he started touching my back. I found a cartoon on the looney tunes channel I played. He moved over to the other side of the bed and told me I could lay back as well. My heart was beating fast from being nervous. "Do you know how to give massages?" he asked. "No, what's that?" "You have to get on top of me so I can show you." Grabbing my arm guiding me on him he took my left leg and pulled it over his waist. Both of my legs were to each side of his waist and he lifted up his shirt. Turning my head to the wall I was afraid to look him in the face. "Give me your hands," he said. Placing both on his left and right nipple. "Mo-mo, you okay?" I nodded my head up and down. "Why are you looking over there? Look at me!" He chuckled. Moving my neck slowly to face him he put his hands on top of mine moving them in circular motion. "See that's all you have to do," moving his hands away. I could feel his dick jumping as my vagina was sitting on top of him. He made sure he placed me right on top of it. "What's that?" I asked. "That's something that happens when boys are happy. You want to touch it?" He asked. Shaking my head side to side saying no. "It's between you and me I won't tell anyone and you can't either, especially not Shawnta. It's going to be our little secret, ok?" He said. I looked at him and said "Ok." "Give me a hug" with excitement in his voice, "You're my favorite." Pulling me forward to him we were chest to chest. He put his hands up my nightgown feeling for my underwear. I didn't say a word while laying on his chest. As he pulled down my panties to my feet. Breathing hard in my ear he pulled down his blue sweatpants from earlier. Goosebumps covering my body he rubbed his hand on my butt. "Sit up," whispering, "let me look at you." Looking at the ceiling avoiding eye contact. He put his hands on my waist grinding my private on his dick. The tingling sensation from my private made me feel like I had to pee. His eyes rolling in the back of his head with moans coming out his mouth you could tell he was enjoying it. I could hear footsteps from the ceiling. I tapped his arm and pointed my finger up.

"Mo? Mo-mo where are you?"

Quickly pushing me off of him pulling his pants up. "Mo, are you down there?" He panicked and yelled "Yeah, Tae we down here." Discreetly telling me to put my panties on as I sat on the end of the bed. "You can come down." "I was looking for you, did you hear me calling you?" Shawnta asked me. "No, I was sitting here watching looney tunes." I lied. Chewing the rest of the tootsies fruit rolls he handed me. "You can watch tv with us if you want." Luke said. "We gotta call mama, she said to call her before we go to sleep and I'm sleepy come on Mo-mo." She grabbed my hand and I followed her upstairs. Luke standing at the end of the stairs saying goodnight to us. When I turned to say it back only to see that he had his finger up to his lips shushing me. "Why were you down there so long?" she asked. Biting my nails confused on how to answer, trying not to say the wrong thing. "Nothing, just sitting there watching tv" I said walking to my bed to sit down. Changing the subject fast, "Can we call mama now so I can make her come home?" I asked. I didn't understand what had just happened but what I did know was I was ready for my mama to come home.

The volume was loud. All you could hear was the loud music in the background and her screaming "HELLO HELLO!" Then hung up the phone. "Call back again." "No, she can't hear us." "I don't care, can I just leave her a message?" This time I got her voicemail "Hey you've reached Tommy. Sorry I missed your call. Leave a message," "Mama, can you come home now?" with salty tears flowing from my eyes "I want you to come back home." I said. Shawnta snatched the phone out my hand, "what are you crying for?" She yelled. I shouted "Leave me alone Tae," tucking myself under my cover. "I want momma." I cried myself to sleep.

The bright light from morning sunrise woke me up. Taking my head from under the cover I looked over to see if Tae was up yet? Legs were hanging halfway off her bed snoring. I continued to lay in my bed thinking about what happened last night. I had to pee so bad but was too nervous to get up. I didn't know how to feel. Got up from my bed and tapped Shawnta so she could walk with me to the bathroom. "Shawnta, can you come to the bathroom with me? I'm scared." I said whispering as if someone else could hear me. "Whhhaaatt? Mo-mo leave me alone, it's light outside you don't need me." Shawnta said annoyed. "I'm going to pee on myself if you don't come please!"I begged. "Girl, you. Oh my gosh. Dang, come on," She finally got up with irritation in her voice.

Following me to the bathroom each step down sounded like a four hundred pound person getting ready to break through. I hate these stairs you couldn't sneak down even if you tried. Passing Grandma Dawn's room I could tell she didn't come home last night cause her bed was still made up perfect. Mama's room door was closed. I assumed she was back but had company. Sitting on the cold toilet made me pee fast. When I looked down it looked like I had dried up milk stains in my panties. Hmm, that's weird, I've never seen that before. Wiping myself then flushing the toilet to wash my hands. When I opened the door Tae had gone back upstairs. I knocked at mama's door to see if she was up but got no answer. I cracked the door open a little, "Mama you up?" I pushed the door open and looked at the bed she wasn't inside. I was puzzled! She really didn't come home last night rushing up the stairs. "Shawnta, mama is not in her room!" Half asleep. "She'll be back soon, it's morning." "Can you get the house phone to call her?"I asked. "NO!" she shouted "It's seven o'clock in the morning," and went back to sleep. Pouting, throwing my body to the bed, It was too bright for me to go back to sleep. I wanted to go downstairs to watch cartoons so she wouldn't get mad if I turned on the tv while she's sleeping. I couldn't get myself up to go down there because I was scared. I didn't know what to expect. I just knew I wasn't ready to face him. I got the courage to run down to grab the house phone from the dining room table. I went through the call log and dialed her number, but all I kept getting was that damn Jill Scott voicemail. I called a few more times then left a message, "Mama, I thought you said you were coming home. Where are you?" and hung up the phone. As I was walking back to my room I could hear the footsteps coming up the basement stairs. I quietly sped up two stairs at a time to get back to my bed. I could hear him stopping at the stairs to see if he heard anything. Then went into the bathroom afterward. The bathroom door opened up quietly. It was like he didn't want to be heard coming out. I put my head under the cover and hid just in case he decided to peek up the stairs. I could hear him tip toeing past our room door again. Silence filled the house and you could hear the beeping noise from the smoke detectors. The vibration from the windows, you could tell someone was knocking at the front door. Uncle Luke yelling "Who is it?" "Open the door, Sugarman it's me!" Grandma yelled

"Where's your key? I told you I wasn't letting you in."He yelled back. Shouting from the porch, "Boy, fuck you. Open the mother fucking door I live here." She yelled back. All the yelling from them woke Shawnta back up. "Who's arguing?" She asked. Taking my head from under the covers, "Uncle Luke and Grandma Dawn. He won't let her in." The bangs from the door startled her. She hopped out the bed rushing downstairs and I followed.

"What's wrong with Grandma? Why is she banging on the door, Luke?" She asked. "She can't come in Shawnta, your mama said not to let her in." Luke said.

"Why? Just open the door, Luke."

"NO!"

"Ough, I can't stand you, I'm about to call mama!"

"I don't care, take your grown self back upstairs."

"Mo, can you grab the phone?" Shawnta asked me. She shrugged her shoulders and stomped on the way up. I took the phone from the base and gave it to her while he continued yelling "Dawn, get off the porch and go back wherever you were." Mama answered the phone when she called "Hello"

"MA! Uncle Luke won't let grandma in. He locked her out and she was banging on the door."Shawnta told. "Ok, I'm about to come home shortly. Where's Mo-Mo?" She asked

"She right here."

"Let me talk to her." I grabbed the phone, "Mama, are you coming home? I thought you said you would be home last night." I said. Sounding like she was still half asleep "Yeah, I'm getting ready to come back. Go eat something I'll see y'all in a minute." Hanging up the phone looking at Shawnta. "She said to go eat something and she'll be home in a minute." Luke came rushing up the stairs saying "you can't tell on me. I'm an adult, little girl, so give me that phone." "I can call my mama if I want too. This is our house, why don't you just leave." Anger in his eyes, "I don't like you and I'm not watching you anymore." I just knew if he had the chance to hit her he would've done so. He went back down stairs then slammed our room door. "Why does she leave us here with him? I hate him so much." Looking at the alarm clock on my dresser I can't believe it's nine o'clock and she still isn't home. "I'm hungry Shawnta. Let's go make some cereal." We went down together into the kitchen, grabbed our bowls and sat at the table. "It's only Apple Jacks and Raisin Brand which one you want?" "Apple Jacks. I don't like that one. The raisins look like brown bugs." I got the milk out of the fridge for us while she grabbed the spoons. As we were eating he came up to the kitchen and took the box of Apple Jacks from in front of us and poured the rest into a bowl. Shawnta smacked her lips. I tapped her on the leg nodding my head. His back was to ours standing at the stove. I'm guessing he didn't hear it. When she got done he told her to go upstairs for smacking her lips. She looked at him and screamed "I HATE YOU" and began to cry. He started laughing in her face and sat down at the table with me. I kept my head down looking at the floating cereal inside my bowl. "What's wrong with you Mo-Mo? Why do you have your head down?" "Y'all are always being mean to each other." I said. "I'm not mean she just doesn't like me, but you're my favorite. You always listen and you're very good and smile at me." I got up to pour my milk in the sink. I didn't want to drink it in front of him. "If you want to come downstairs with me you can." I nodded my head and headed back up with Tae. I sat on her bed next to her and asked her "Are you okay?" "Leave me alone Mo, I don't feel like talking." She said. "Maybe you should try to get along with him and be nice." "Never will I like him. He shouldn't even be here." I turned the tv on and put on the CatDog cartoon for us. She began to lay back on her bed and I laid the opposite way. She giggled loudly when she saw the cat and dog were connected as one. "How is that possible?" I chuckled. "I don't think that's possible. This is fake." We laughed together. "Monique," Luke shouted "When you are done watching your movie come here for a minute." "Why does he want you to come down there?" "I'm not sure I didn't do anything wrong." "Go see what he wants, then come back and tell me what happened." I nervously came down the stairs as I looked around for him. Cautiously waiting for him to jump out to scare me or something. I called his name but no response. Then faintly I heard him call out my name. At that moment I knew he was downstairs waiting for me. I began tiptoeing down the large steps trying not to fall between the gaps in the stairs. When I got to the basement I noticed he randomly turned off his room light. It startled me so I froze. He softly said "Moniquee, come here." Heart racing asking him "Where are you?" "I'm right here, just come behind the sheet." I gently moved the sheet back. All I saw was his silhouette. Before I could blink there was his long arm reaching for my hand. He snatched me and lifted me onto his lap. I could already tell he was horny because his dick was poking me through his pajama pants. He hugged me like he missed me then threw my arms over his shoulders making me hug him back. He began grinding me, rocking me back and forth. I could feel his cheeks up against mine. His lips on my right ear moans coming from his mouth. Making me feel tingly and warm inside. Slightly lifting my small body up pulling my panties slowly down my legs. He pulled his pajama pants down to his knees and laid back on the bed. Grabbing my hand leading me upon him again. He pulled each leg of mine towards him making sure they were completely open. "Can we do the same thing as last night?" he asked me. "Uh huh," I shrugged carelessly. "Okay, I'm going to guide you the same way you don't have to do anything." His penis was so hard it was difficult for him to lay flat on his stomach. He made sure my private sat right on his tip. He moaned out "Oh my god," he moaned, placing each of his hands on my buttcheeks. The tingling sensation flowed through my private area again. I got that wet feeling from before. I felt like I had to pee. I quietly said, "I have to pee Luke." Getting more aroused by what I said he lifted me up then laid me on my back and opened my legs. He crouched on his knees over me. "Owww don't worry about that, that's how it's supposed to be." Suddenly I felt a lot of wet stuff falling on top of my vagina. Snatching the white t-shirt off of him he began wiping whatever that was off of me. Sliding off the bed, putting his pants back on, handing mine to me. "Hurry up, you've been down here for a while now." Tiredly saying "Come on it's time for you to go back upstairs." I got up from the bed looking for my panties on the floor. "Can you turn the light on?" "What are you looking for?" "My underwear," I said, reaching into his pocket. I pushed the sheet back to go up the stairs. "Hey Mo," I turned my head looking him in the face. "Remember what I said, don't tell anybody, not even Tae." I nodded my head and continued to walk up the stairs. I went into the bathroom because my coochie felt so weird. I sat down on the toilet to pull down my panties. It was that gooey stuff again. I took some tissue to wipe it off then flushed it. I was too small to look in the mirror at myself. I was so confused about why he kept saying don't tell anybody. When I opened the bathroom door he was standing in the hallway. I jumped back because I didn't know he was out there. He laughed, "What's wrong with you? Why are you so jumpy?" I gave no response and quickly ran up the stairs. "What happened, why were you down there so long?" "I had to do number two when I was in the bathroom." "Oh, did he say anything while you were down there?" I paused for a minute. I just knew he was listening. Trying not to give her eye contact, "Yeah he told me to tell you to stop being so mean to him." Smacking her lips "Yeah, whatever. He's mean to me so I'm mean to him. Don't nobody wants to be his friend anyway." I went over to the toy box and grabbed a few barbies to play with on the floor. I heard Luke coming up the stairs looking at us both "Y'all okay?" Shawnta stared at him for a moment before she said "We're fine." "Alright, I just wanted to check on y'all. Your momma called to say she would be here shortly."

My eyes blew up from excitement. I was beyond ready for her to come home. "Well, I'm about to make some noodles if y'all want some." With a smirk on his face, "I know you want some Tae so you can drown them in hot sauce. Better hurry up before she makes it home cause you know she's going to be mad." They both began to laugh. After he walked downstairs Tae said, "He's just trying to be nice because mama is on her way." She got up quickly and ran down the stairs. I didn't move from the floor.

Only thing I could think of at that moment was him putting that wet stuff on me. So much curiosity wondering did he pee on me and if he did why would he do that? Hmm, he really likes me to be on him chuckling to myself with the barbies in my hand. I began playing out the things he did in the basement with the toys. Taking the toy clothes off of them, putting one doll on top of the other. I could hear my name being called but I didn't answer. "You don't want any noodles?" Shouting "No, I'm not hungry." Glancing over to the side of my bed. I saw my medium size brown teddy bear on the floor. I slid across the floor to grab it. I got on top of it and began to grind. I was curious if I could make myself have that feeling again. I quickly got up when I heard footsteps. "What are you doing?" Tae asked. "Nothing, playing with the toys." "Are you okay? You're acting weird." "Weird, what does that mean?" "Forget it. You didn't want any noodles?" "No, I'm not hungry right now. Let's straighten up before mama gets here." She giggled out loud, "what are those barbies doing? Why is one on top of the other like that?" "I don't know," quickly throwing them into the toybox. "You shouldn't do that, it looks nasty," She said. Pouting pushing the bear under my bed. "Sounds like mama just pulled in the driveway." I said excited.

You could hear the rattling on her car whenever she pulled up. By that time I rushed downstairs to meet her at the backdoor. She had just opened the door. "Mama!" "Dang, you were waiting for me at the door, huh?" "Yes, I missed you!" Reaching her arms out to give us a hug. "Why were you gone so long?" "I was out taking care of business this morning." Even though I already knew she wasn't telling the truth. It didn't matter because she made it back home. "What's up sis?" Luke walked up asking. "Hey, thanks for watching the girls for me." She responded "Oh, nah, you're good big sis. You know I'll do anything to help while I'm here." "Well, I appreciate it since I can't depend on my mama. Did they give you a hard time?" Looking over at Shawnta with a thinking face then smirked, "No, they were good." "What did y'all eat? Did you starve my babies?" with a grin on her face? "Man, of course not they just had some noodles. Well, Shawnta did. Mo-Mo didn't want any." "Ok, let me get out of this kitchen. I need to shower. I've been in these clothes since yesterday." She said, "Can we go outside today?" We begged. "Wait until I'm out of the shower." Having her back home was a refresher. I was tired of sitting upstairs. "I'm about to watch cartoons down here." I said. "Yeah, me too," Shawnta said.

Luke sat down at the table looking across the room glancing at us like he was watching tv too. I think he was worried about me saying something to Shawnta. He kept looking over at me whenever my lips moved. It was confusing only because I could have told her everything upstairs. I'm beyond afraid to even say something. He gave me anxiety. I felt like my every move I made was being watched. Glued to the couch holding my urine. I refused to get up until he went back down to the basement. I yelled out to mama purposely to see if she had come out of the bathroom. He would act like he was scared of mama. He didn't sit in here long. I knew when she came out he would eventually go down to his room. Shouting from the cracked door "Yeah, I'm about to come out now. Shawnta is Luke downstairs?" "No, he's still at the table." "Nigga you don't need to see me in a towel go downstairs!" "Ain't nobody looking at you, man" he blurted out walking through the kitchen. He was really starting to creep me out. After she got dressed she came to the front room with excitement in her voice. Let's go over to Auntie house so y'all can play with the kids since everybody over there. Jumping up fast "Yay, yes I'm ready to go!" I screamed with excitement "Well, you have to get in the shower first. Both of you have been in pajamas since last night. It's now three o'clock in the afternoon. Mo, you go first since you like to take forever." I hurried up the stairs to get a face rag and towel. When I got into the bathroom she was sitting on the toilet while the water was filling up the tub waiting for me. "Come take your clothes off so I can wash you up." I paused for a moment, startled. "Huh?" "I said take your clothes off. What are you waiting for?" with aggression in her voice. Pulling my gown above my head then pulling down my underwear to the floor. "Come here and let me smell you. Sniffing my underarms oh you still have some time before you get musty. Go ahead and get in." I saw her reaching for my panties on the floor as I sat down in the tub. She picked them up and looked inside and sniffed. She looked over at me saying "What is this?" Showing me the inside of my panties. I began to Quiver. I don't know if I didn't use the bathroom on myself. "Hmm, you're too young to be having this" and tossed them down the dirty clothes shoot. She began to soap up the rug and told me to stand up. Starting at my back down to my butt then the back of my legs. Squat and open your legs. "Owch!" "What?" "It hurts when you do that." "Sorry, I have to clean it all the way." Pouring water over my body to wash the soap away. I was lost in my space. She giggled to herself "Mo, are you okay?" Her motherly words were pulling the emotions out of me. I thought to myself I really wanted to tell her everything, but my lips wouldn't allow me to speak. I snapped out of it and told her I was okay. She got me out of the tub and told me to go into her room to get lotioned up then dressed. I went upstairs to put on my shoes as I waited for Tae to get out of the shower. After she was dressed we got ready to head out the backdoor. Mama yelled down the stairs to Luke, "You want to come with us? It's not good to be isolated in your room." "No, I'm good. I don't feel like going anywhere." In a concerned voice "You should at least want to be around other family and people, but I guess we'll be back later!" A breath of fresh air around my cousins was all I needed. Pure sunshine and fun could make me forget about everything that happened last night and this morning. I got into the backseat and put on my seatbelt while Shawnta got in the front. Pulling off from the house cruising to the main street where we saw Mike and Marty at the corner. Mike waved his hand at her. She turned her head and steering wheel to the right. We headed down Outer Drive passing all the nicer looking houses. "Oww, momma these houses are big and pretty." "Yeah, they are." Turning on the block where all my cousins lived. Everyone was outside. Some of my older cousins were standing in front of their cars smoking and drinking. As the younger ones our age were running up and down the street. When they saw us they began yelling "Mo-Mo" and "Shawnta." I was excited to see them. My cousins Chen, Terry, Devon, Victoria, Mika ran up to the car as I got out the backseat. "Come on y'all so we can play freeze tag." "What's up family," Momma said. "Ayee, what's up Tommy," everyone replied. The loud hip-hop music filled the block. The next time we move we'll be moving into this area. You would have thought it was a party outside from how many of us were out. "Me and Shawnta will be the freezers since we're older y'all can run and hide," said Mika. Me and Victoria ran down the block towards her house to hide in the backyard. Chen, Devon made their way down to us. When they figured out we were nowhere near them, they came running down the street. "We got y'all now!" they yelled out. Aunt Lola, Victoria and Mika's mom came to the door as we ran past Tae. "Y'all be careful running by that street." Chen's mom yelled out for her to come back in front of their house. We began to race each other. Momma shouted "we won't be here too long so play yourselves out." I was saddened when it was time to go back. All those uncomfortable feelings I wanted to stay gone came back, but there was nothing I could do, but get in the car and keep the secrets.

Chapter 4

Secrets in Me

BEEP BEEP BEEP...... I could hear the sound echoing through my head. Oh my goodness it's morning already? Wiping the crusties from my eyes, pulling the cover over my head. I felt like I barely slept with that annoying alarm clock making all that noise. How can something so small make that much noise? The longer you let it beep the louder it gets. "Oh my goodness, Shawnta, please turn it off, it's too loud!" We know it's Monday already ugh! Mama's footsteps approaching the door, "Tae and Mo-Mo are y'all up?" Yelling again, "Y'all get up. I gotta get ready for work, so come on down." Stretching at the end of my bed before I stood up. "I'm up," in a fuzzy voice Shawnta, "come on we have to go downstairs." "Ok dang, I heard her for the first time." Rushing down the stairs to get in the bathroom first because mama took forever fixing her hair and stuff. I washed and brushed my teeth and went into the kitchen to make myself a bowl of cereal. I'd rather eat before I get dressed just in case I make a mess. Mama brushed past me while sitting at the table. She yelled Luke's name from the stairs to get up. It was time for her to leave and she wanted him to walk us to school. I could hear the irritation in his response shouting back, "Alright I hear you." "Shawnta, I guess you're not hungry, it's almost seven-thirty and you haven't made it to the kitchen," said mama. "Here I come." She put on her shoes as she sat down at the table. Grabbing her folder and purse heading out the door. "I'll see y'all later be good and have a good day at school." After I finished my cereal I got up from the table and ran to put my clothes on then to get my book bag from upstairs. Luke, yawning loudly walking up the stairs, "Are y'all ready?" "I'm almost done eating," said Shawnta. "Well you should've been done already, it's damn near time to go. Hurry up." Rushing down putting on my sweater, "Here I am." I sat down on the couch. She hadn't gotten done with her cereal yet. With an attitude, "When I come out from the bathroom you should be done!"Luke yelled. I went into the kitchen and sat next to her quietly saying, "Hurry up so we can go." He seemed to be irritated and I didn't want him to get upset with her. She drank her milk as fast as she could and put her bowl in the sink. When he walked out the bathroom we were already standing by the door. His demeanor was completely off. We knew he didn't want to walk us. Something must have been bothering him. "Shit, gotta grab my keys y'all go ahead to get a headstart" he said. As we walked out the door the warm air blew past my face. I could smell the rain coming as I looked to the sky. It was such a gloomy morning. You could hear him slamming the door from a few houses down. Echoing down the block "I'm behind y'all." Shawnta began to walk faster after she heard him. As we approached the end of the block we got ready to cross the main street. She grabbed my right hand and said, "Are you ready to run?" "Wait, I have to watch y'all cross the street." Pretending like we didn't hear him. I looked one way as she looked the other way, "One, two, three!" We ran to the other side of the street in front of the store. He yelled out loudly in anger, "Don't do that again. Y'all supposed to cross with me!" He followed us while on the opposite side of the street two blocks over. The crossing guard was at the next corner to guide us over and into the school. When I looked over for him he was standing in front of the funeral home watching. As we walked into the left side of the school. He waved goodbye. Our lockers were on the same floor but in different hallways. After I put my coat up Shawnta walked me to my classroom before she went to her side of the building. "I'll meet you back at your locker when school is out to get you." She said. My teacher was at the door to greet everyone coming in to be seated. I was happy to be back in school. Especially since I met a new friend. When I walked in she was already sitting at the table. The closer I got I saw her looking at me smiling. "I was waiting for you." She said. "Hi Cassie," I smiled back. "Where were you?" "Why?" "I didn't want anyone to take your seat plus I wanted to talk about our weekend." I knew she didn't have many friends. The kids in the class made fun of her lazy eye and crooked teeth. They would even make jokes about how high she wore her uniform pants. I couldn't see how others viewed her because her personality was bright. We would go into the bathroom during break and lock the door just to throw wet paper towel balls to the ceiling then watch them stick. When it was downtime in the classroom we would lay our heads towards one another. Wherever I went she was always beside me. She offered me some of her food at lunchtime even though I had my own. The teacher gave the class one more bathroom break before school let out. Only two could go in at a time. Cassie and I were at the end of the line so we were last to go. Mrs. Gardner began to direct everyone back to the room once the two girls before us came out. She instructed us to go ahead and return once we are done. I went into the first stall while she was in the one beside me. I stormed to the sink to wash my hands. Trying to get back to class fast. "Cassie, come on we gotta get back." She came out buckling her belt while coming to the sink. She reached for the paper towel to dry her hands. I walked to the door and waited for her. Looking at me she asked, "Have you ever been kissed before?" "No, have you kissed?" Giggling, "No I haven't but do you want to try it?" "Are you going to tell anyone?" Surprisingly she said, "No, it's our secret. I promise!" "Let's pinky swear on it." We took our pinky fingers and shook to never mention. She put her body close to mine so that we were face to face. As she leaned forward her glossy lips touched mine. I felt the same sensation from the weekend. A feeling of shock. I can't believe I'm kissing a girl. Thinking about what Shawnta said about the two dolls. I jumped back, I looked at her and walked out the bathroom.

Rushing to my seat as I entered the classroom I put my head down when I saw her coming. When she sat down beside me I looked the other way. Whispering to me, "Are you mad at me?" SHe said. I pretended as if I didn't hear her. She tapped my arm but I moved it away. My nerves were going crazy and felt like I was turning red. I didn't know how to feel afterwards. So anxious for the bell to ring. I tried my hardest to keep myself from looking at her. Hoping that Tae would be at the locker so we could leave right out. Mrs. Gardner began calling table by table to line up by the door to avoid everyone rushing up at once. When she called our table next Cassie jumped up and fled to the line. I could tell she was upset about me ignoring her. I wasn't trying to be mean, it's just that I didn't know how to feel after that kiss. You could hear the classroom doors opening as the bell rang. The hallways flooded like a silent tsunami when the students came out. I thought Cassie sprinted to her locker then left because I didn't see her once I got to mine. Shawnta was no where to be found. Looking from one end of the hallway to the other. I grabbed my jacket and book bag and began walking towards the exit door. Cassie and Tae were standing out by the gate. "Why didn't you wait for me Tae?" "My teacher let us out five minutes before the bell rang! There were too many people in the hallway anyway." Rolling my eyes glancing at Cassie, "When did you get out here?" "I didn't have to stop at my locker," She said as she rolled her eyes. "Alright, let's go then." Tae caught up with her friends as we followed behind. "Are you mad at me?" she asked. "No, I'm not, you did nothing wrong." "So, why were you being mean?" "Honestly, I don't know if I was just nervous." "Well, we pinky promised we would never say anything, right?" "Yeah, it's between us." She grinned and I smiled back. We were one block away from the corner store. I blurted "Shawnta, let's go get something out of the store." "I only have seventy-five cents," she said. "Can you get me a bag of chips or candy?" "Yeah, man." "I have two dollars if you want a dollar. Here," said Cassie. "That's your money, keep it." I said."No, it's okay I want you to have it." Grinning with my right cheek up, "Well, thank you." I was blushing hard. When we arrived at the store I grabbed a small bag of hot Cheetos and four packs of now and laters. "I don't have enough money for all that Mo-Mo, get one thing," said Shawnta. "Cassie gave me a dollar. I'm buying my own stuff now!" "Good more stuff for me," she laughed. We paid for our stuff while Cassie and the other kids waited outside. Once Shawnta and I walked out the store everyone started walking towards the bridge. I walked with Cassie to the light and we gave each other a hug. "Come on Mo, we have to get home. Uncle Luke is waiting for us!" We grabbed each other's hands as we ran across the street. "See y'all tomorrow," we said loudly. Opening my pack of banana now and laters as we approached the house. I didn't see Uncle Luke coming from the porch to see us down. There he was standing at the front door waiting for us. He opened the door as Shawnta walked in first. Neither one of them spoke a word. "Hey, Mo how was school?" he asked. I slouched my head down. "It was good." "Do you have homework? I can help you with it!" "No, my teacher didn't give out any today." "Mo come take your school clothes off," Shawnta shouted from the stairs. He touched my shoulder as I took my coat off and hung it in the front closet. I didn't bother to look at him. I grabbed my backpack from the floor and walked upstairs. He slowly followed behind me. "Y'all hungry?" Shawnta sitting on the edge of her bed looking at me for a response. "No," facing the opposite direction from where he was standing. "We stopped at the store to get junk food." "Well y'all know you have to wait until you eat something first." "Why?" Shawnta asked loudly. "Don't question me, I'm grown. You're a kid," he shouted. "You're not an adult, you're only seventeen." "Shut up! You talk too much, you're not grown." When I glanced over to her I could see the tears filled in her eyes. "Yeah, don't cry now, stop talking to me like you my mom or something." "I hate you," she screamed. He walked over to her bed and snatched her bag of snacks. She began screaming and crying. "I'm telling my momma. Get out of our house you don't live here nobody wants you here!" "You're lucky I can't whoop you," said Luke. "That's why I'm going to tell my momma Mo was in the basement with you!" The look on his face I knew if he had the permission to he would've beaten her for sure. "You can get your stuff back when your momma gets here," as he stormed downstairs. "Don't cry Tae," I said. "No, I hate him," as she continued to cry out. I went over to turn on some cartoons just to calm her down. I stayed on the floor in front of her bed. "I can't wait until he leaves." I said. "Momma said he won't be here too long, don't worry Tae." "Why is he always nice to you, but mean to me?" She asked. I shrugged my shoulders and shook my head. I felt bad for her because I didn't understand why he treated her like she did something to him, but not me. The room was filled with silence. I just stared at the TV. Eventually Tae dozed off taking a nap. I wasn't sleepy, but I didn't want him to come up and only see that I was awake; so I got into the bed with her and closed my eyes. We must've slept for an hour. Luke yelled up the stairs, "Y'all come down and eat." Neither of us responded to him. I opened one eye because I heard him coming up the stairs. "Mo get up so you can eat something. Your momma will be home soon." "Ok," I got up from the bed and followed him downstairs. "You want some fishsticks and fries?" "Yes." "It's almost done. It's in the oven now." I sat at the kitchen table as he grabbed a plate from the cabinet. He went back to the stairs and called out to Tae to come down. "Get up, Shawnta, it's time to eat." "Alright, here I come!" He came back into the kitchen and made our plates. "I hope you woke up with a better attitude," he said. She ignored him. "Oh I guess you're still mad at me for taking your junk food. You can have it back. I don't want it." Scooting her chair to the table. "It's cool you don't have to talk to me," while giggling to himself. Placing our plates in the sink after gobbling down our food. We sat back down and began to eat our snacks. Shawnta, was acting goofy, doing anything to make me laugh. She stuck her head in the kitchen chair and got stuck. "Stop playing, get your head out silly." I laughed so hard my stomach was tight. "What's so funny?" Luke asked coming from the living room. "I'm stuck, get me out!" Holding his belly laughing loudly. "Nope, you got it, get yourself out. Why would you put your head through there anyway?" He asked. "I can't," as she pulled. She began to cry, that's when I knew she was serious. Stomping her feet, smacking her hands on the table "Get me out!" It wasn't funny anymore. "Uncle Luke, help her!" He continued to make fun of her. "I bet you won't do that again. Say please!" "Please! My neck hurt," she cried out. It was like he enjoyed seeing her cry. My heart began beating fast and I was anxious. I shouted, "Help her now!" Pushing her head up to the open space pulling her head out. "Now, don't do that again!" "Oww," slamming herself to the chair, "it's not funny!" "You'll be alright, you shouldn't have been playing." I was annoyed with him. Getting up from the table, stomping up the stairs. I couldn't wait until momma got home.

Throwing myself on my bed. I wasn't going back down. Shawnta, didn't come up after me. I waited a few moments before I went down to check on her. I didn't hear anymore sobbing. I thought she may have been in the bathroom. I quietly creeped down the stairs into the hallway, but the bathroom door was wide open. So, she wasn't in here. Peeped my head to the living room and kitchen, but she wasn't there either. I stood at the basement top stair. It was very quiet. "Shawnta!" I called out. Got no answer. "Tae! Yeah, are you okay?" "Yeah," with a cracky voice she responded. "Are you coming up?" Uncle Luke said, "Yes she's coming." I went and sat on the couch to wait for her. It was a few moments before she came up though. From the strange look on her face. I knew he had done the same thing to her as he did to me. She didn't even look my way, however she went straight to the bathroom. I got up and went to our room. As she sat on her bed she seemed so spaced out. "Are you okay?" I asked. She ignored me and laid down. "Mo," she said. "Yes?" "Don't go downstairs anymore." "Did something happen Tae?" She went mute and didn't say another word until momma made it home.

Chapter 5

Is This Right

"Nisha and the girls are coming over today," said momma. She's one of mom's childhood friends. "Yayyy! We can pull out the Barbie dream house to play with." That meant they were going to have grown up talks with drinks. "Make sure that room is clean. I don't want to see anything on the floor." Momma said. I didn't have to do anything other than make my bed since the room was clean already. I was looking forward to them coming over since we weren't on good terms with our friends. "Beep beep", I heard the horn from upstairs. I went to the window and looked out and saw their car parked in front of the house. Nisha and her daughter Nae were getting out of the car. I could hear my momma opening the door. "Hey, girl what's up! Mo, come down and say hi to Nisha." Sprinting down to the living room. "Hey Nisha and Nae." "Hey Mo!" they replied. "You're getting so big and pretty!" "Thank you." I said. They sat down on the couch while momma turned on the music videos on TV. "You wanna play with the Barbie Dream house I have in my room?"I asked Nae. "Momma, can I go play with toys with Mo?" I asked. "Yes you can." Nae followed me to my room. I pulled out the house from one of the closets. "Dang that's big," she said. "I got it for Christmas. It has a pool and elevator on it." "That's sweet," she said with excitement. "Are you going to show me how it works?" Yeah, grabbing the Barbie's out the toy box. I had four Barbie's, two white with blonde hair and the other two were brown with black hair. "Here. Pick which one you want to be." She chose from one of the black dolls, so did I. I began to show her how to operate a battery oper-ated elevator. I had a bottle of water next to my bed that I poured into the toy pool. We began talking and acting like we were Barbie's. "Let's get in the pool!" "Wait! We have to get undressed first. Well I don't have my swim-suit." "It's okay we can just be naked." I didn't think anything was wrong with our dolls being naked. It's not like we were.

"Y'all alright up there?" Momma asked. "Yes, we're playing with the Barbie house." "Okay." We took the clothes off of them and put them into the water. Laugh-ing loudly, "The water is so cold." Putting them under water. "Let's get out and dry off. We have to take the elevator to the room." I pressed the button to have the elevator go up. "Hey. Follow me," I said. "This is my room with a huge bed." She took her doll and pretended as she was jumping on it. So I did the same with mine. She laid her Barbie back and I jumped on top of hers with mine. Giggling, "What are you doing?" She said, "We're playing house." "But there's no boy dolls to do that." "So we can use these ones." We started acting out every-thing we did to the Barbies with each other. The room was extremely quiet. She got on top of me and started humping me. Then it was my turn. I did it exactly how Uncle Luke taught me. It went on for a few moments. Then I heard cracks from the stairs like someone was creeping up. When I turned my head to the left I saw my momma face!

"What in the fuck are you doing Mo-Mo!" She screamed out! "Nisha! I'm about to beat the hell out of this girl!" "What Tommy? What happened?" "I just caught them humping!" "What the fuck NAE!" "What are you doing up here! Come on now! We're about to go!" My heart was beating so fast! I was terrified and trembling. I began to cry and so did Nae. "Momma, I didn't do anything," crying as she walked past my mom down the stairs. "Bring your ass down here Mo you're in trouble!" "Tommy girl, I don't know what to say," shaking her head. "No, Nisha I'm sorry I don't even know what to say. I'm about to get to the bottom of this shit. I don't know where she got this from. Mo-Mo that's not how you play, especially not with another girl like you. Do you understand me?" "Yes." My momma was standing there with the belt in her hand. "Alright Nisha, girl, we'll talk later." Nisha popping Nae on her butt with her hand walking out shutting the door. "I'm about to whoop your ass get in here." As she grabbed me by my shirt and pushed me in her room. She began hitting me on my butt with the belt. "Yelling where and who did you get this from?" Crying and screaming out, "I don't know! Nobody!" "Tell me the truth now," hitting me more. "I promise momma I don't know." Hitting me harder, "That's not how you play! That shit is nasty!" Hitting me more I yelled louder, "OK! Ok, OK!" "I better not ever catch you doing no shit like that again." Hitting me really hard for the last time now and telling me to get upstairs. I laid across my bed wiping the tears from my face. Thinking to myself why didn't I just tell her Uncle Luke did this to me? I just couldn't bring myself to tell her. I knew I was supposed to keep it a secret, but I didn't know I would get in trouble for doing it. This is so unfair. Knowing what I know now I wish I would've opened my mouth then because it could've put an end to everything that continued. This is so unfair I just cried myself to sleep. When I woke up I continued to lay there. I was embarrassed. I didn't want my momma to even look at me. Shawnta was back from riding bikes. "What's wrong with you? Why are you up here?" I didn't say anything back. I was ashamed to even say what had happened. "Hello? Why are you just laying there? Ma!" She blurted out. "What's wrong with Mo." I sat up against my headboard as I heard her coming up. She closed the room door behind her. Standing in the middle of the room looking at us both. "I don't care which one of y'all tell me, but one of y'all better tell me something," with aggression. Shawnta standing by her bed looking confused. "Tae, you weren't here, but Mo and Nae were caught humping on each other earlier. Do you know anything about that?" "No," she responded quickly. "I don't do that." "Well, have you seen anybody doing that or have it been done to you before?" Shaking her head back and forth, no. "Look at me Mo! Where did you get that from?" "Nowhere." "Who have you seen do that type of stuff?" "Nobody momma." She shook her head with her hands on her hips saying, "If I find out that one of y'all been doing this or someone has done that to you and neither of you told me it's going to be a fucking problem. Do y'all understand me?" "Yes." "You're on punishment. Don't come out of this room unless you have to use the bathroom or eat!" I could tell she was angry and highly upset. After she went back down, Tae quickly asked me, "What did you do?" I just turned my head in shame.

A few days later, Uncle Luke saw me in the living room watching tv. He laughed and asked, "What did you do to get in trouble?" I didn't think it was funny so I stared and ignored him. "Why did you do that? You know you're not supposed to be doing that," he chuckled. "That's not what two girls do, only a boy and a girl do things like that." He giggled and walked away. I should've told what happened in that basement since he thought it was funny for me to get in trouble about something he showed me. I was confused. How was I supposed to know two girls weren't supposed to do things like that? I was glad to be off punishment. Being in that room for days and not being able to do anything became boring. Momma said I could go outside. My face lit up with excitement. I ran and put my shoes on then headed out the door. Everyone was outside. Layla, standing out in the front of her house waving for me to come down. Rushing past the girls next door. Neither of us spoke to each other. "I have some chalk to play hopscotch with," she said. She handed me a pink stick while she used blue. She drew the squares and I did the numbers. "Let me go first," she said. We took turns going until we got tired. "I have jump ropes in the garage at home. Let's go in my backyard to jump."I said. "I have to ask my mom, wait here." She took off running to ask her parents. When she came out we raced to the backyard. We had an old red raggedy garage door. It was hard to lift up most of the time. She helped me push it up enough for us to go under. It was only our bikes, a few lawn chairs, and dust everywhere. The sunlight shining in from outside was the only way we could see since there wasn't a light inside. "There it is!" I grabbed the ropes hanging from the long nail. "Come on, it's too dark and hot in here." I said. We jumped against each other. Trying to see who could go the longest without stopping. "Hi Layla," momma was standing at the backdoor asking if we wanted bottles of water. "Yes, please," we responded. She sat them on the concrete porch then closed the door. "I wish I could stay down here forever," said Layla. Sitting down drinking my water, "Really, why? I hate being at home." Isaid. "My mom is so mean all she does is whoop me. Besides, I get tired of watching all my brothers and sisters," she laughed. "I feel like a grown up. I'm only eight and my little brother calls me mama." She said. I honestly didn't know what to say. What could I say I was a kid and it was only me and Tae. I couldn't imagine my momma having more after me and I had to look after them. "Dang, why do your momma always leave you to watch them." I asked. "I don't know, I guess because none of our daddies live with us and I'm the oldest." "Well don't be sad," I said "things will be better soon we all have to grow up. One day you'll be all by yourself and no one to answer to." "I really like you Mo, you're always nice to me," she said. I chuckled blushing with my hand covering my mouth. She whispered, "You would make a nice girlfriend one day. I had a girlfriend once we did stuff together." "Like what?" "I can't tell you it's a secret." "Well, I won't tell anyone I promise. I can keep a secret." "I guess I can show you, but we have to go somewhere no one can see us. Let's go back into the garage." "We have to be quick!" She told me to lay down on the lawn chair she got on top of me leaning forward kissing me on the neck. With my eyes looking to the ceiling I've never done this before. Her grinding on me I was nervous, but liked it. We heard a noise so I pushed her off. Grabbing my bike pushing the door to get out. As she came out she said she needed to go back home. "You want me to come back down with you?" "No, it's okay I'll see you later," walking out the backyard gate. I left my bike on the ground and went inside the house.

From that point on I started to like girls a little. I would rather be with the girl and become a bit obsessive. The block had started calling me Mo-Mo gay gay because we played hide go getto . Basically you hide and the person you find you had to do something with kiss, touch or whatever, but since it was all girls I was called the freaky gay one. Hell, it became so normal for me I didn't care. Layla and I started humping in the garage every time we played. I knew my momma would beat me if she caught me again, but I just didn't care anymore. Luke had me in the basement damn near everyday momma went to work. Showing and doing so much to me. Everything I was taught I did with others. I learned how to have an orgasm at the age of seven. I knew about and how to go down on a man and so much more. That feeling became addictive. I had to hump on pillows and teddy bears whenever it came about.

One time Carl came over for a weekend. He and I were upstairs playing our nintendo 64 while Shawnta was downstairs watching tv. I got tired of playing and grabbed a few toys. He went and laid across my bed. Told me to come here. I slid over from the toy box. He pulled his pants and underwear down enough to pull out his private part. Grabbing my hand putting onto his penis. I snatched away. He began pulling my head to his penis. I continued to pull away, but that didn't stop him. Shoving his stuff in my mouth hard. He began pushing my head down with his hands. Humping my mouth really hard. Gagging feeling like I had to throw up. It made him stop. "Don't tell anybody I'll get in trouble," he said. After pulling his pants and underwear up he continued playing the game. I sat there after wiping my mouth with my towel. Wow, my own brother. I could never say anything about this. I was disgusted and felt an instant hatred for him. I didn't like for him to come over anymore after that. Whenever he did I would get extremely irritated. I thought he was sick in the head and didn't know any better since he had a mental illness. Nevertheless I caught him sneaking into Grandma Dawn's room the next day. I creeped around and followed him. She had to be in a deep sleep from whatever drug she took. She was lying on her right side with the tv on snoring. He sat on the floor next to her bed in front of the tv. I saw him pull her white panties down and began to feel all over her butt cheeks. From the looks of it he was excited and did it for a while. He put one hand inside of his pants while rubbing on her. She moved a little bit and he ducked down. I rushed back upstairs. This shit had to be normal! How did she not feel him touching all over her? I was outdone. I knew he didn't know I saw him, however I never mentioned it to him or anyone else. Did she pretend like me, or did she like it? Fuck that! That shit wasn't right. That was our grandmother. One day Uncle Luke played hide and seek with us and I hid under Grandma Dawn's bed. I stayed there for a while. I knew Tae hid upstairs. I could hear her footsteps tip toeing. Once I saw Uncle Luke creep up there I came from under the bed. I stood at the bottom stair to see if I heard them. Neither of them said anything. I creeped up slowly. I knew they didn't hear me coming. Put my hand over my mouth to keep me from laughing once I jumped out to scare one of them. Kneeling down on the top stair, I leaned my head forward looking at the room. I saw Luke's long legs and Tae's legs. Peeping back I looked again and stared. He had Shawnta sitting on his lap with her shirt and bra up on my bed. I was in complete shock. I knew he had done something to her in the basement before, but to actually see it, it was unbelievable.

My stomach was turning and had knots in it. She saw me peeping and looked me right in my eyes. It was like she was crying out for help. I did absolutely nothing to stop him. He was caressing her breast with his big hands. She put her head down in shame. I became angry, because she did nothing to stop him from doing things to me. So I sat there and watched a bit longer. Getting off my knees to stand he must have heard the cracks from the stair. He looked over and saw me there. Pulling her shirt and bra down then pushed Tae off of him and quickly stood up. Standing in the hallway of the room I just looked him in the face. "Why are you looking like that Mo?" he said. "Brushing past me saying you didn't see anything right?" Shawnta walked to her bed and sat looking out the window. "Are you okay?" I asked. "Leave me alone Mo-Mo don't say nothing to me." She was angry at me why? I wasn't the one that did anything to her. I sat on my bed and left her alone like she asked. I heard her sobbing over there because the room was so quiet.

My mom had met this guy named Ron that had to be at least ten years older than her. He was short and light skinned like my mom. She invited him over this day and introduced him to me and Shawnta. He dressed in the flyest clothes and stayed in a fresh pair of kicks. He seems like an okay guy, but a fake person eventually takes their mask off. Everytime I go downstairs I'll see a pair of his kicks at the front door. Crazy part is the more he was there the more momma stayed home. He would take her out on dates and give her money to do things with us. He gave her money to take us to Wilzan for a weekend. His family was big. He had three sisters around his age. Laura, had a son (Eric) him and Tae were the same age and (Maya) my age. Betty, she cooked the best food and cheesecake. Her house was laid from top to bottom. Cathy, she was mean, strict, and stuck up. When he and momma got really serious he would take us over his family's houses on the holidays. He was excited to show off my mama. She was young, pretty, with a banging body. He became obsessed with her. Damn near like he wanted her all to himself. If she wasn't with him he didn't want her going out anywhere. Whenever she did she would lie to him and say that we were over to our cousin's house. She came home drunk one night and he called our house phone nonstop, then popped up in the morning. As she was throwing up in a gray mop bucket he was cussing her out. With us listening from the stairs. She kept apologizing for drinking. Why? I didn't understand that she's grown and can do what she wants. "Shut up you're a liar! Why did you lie about where you were Tommy? I rode past your cousin's house and you weren't there nor your car! So, where did you go?" "Ron I'm not lying I swear." We heard bumps and a few yells. There were sounds as if someone was getting thrown against a wall or something. I went down and went into the bathroom. He heard the door close and began to whisper his curse words. I sat on the toilet for a moment then flushed. Turned the water on and pretended to wash my hands.

When I came out I knocked on her door, "Mama are you up?" "Yeah," she responded, "I'll be out in a second. What's wrong?" "I'm hungry." "Okay give me a minute. I'm not feeling well, I'll make you some cereal." "Okay." Before I made it up the stairs Ron came out of the room. "Hey Mo-Mo you alright?" "Hi Ron, yes." "Alright see you later." It took everything out of me to speak back. I know he did something to my mama. I just didn't like him anymore. Whatever happened it took a while for her to come out. I just wanted to see her happy. It was just the beginning of a toxic, possessive, and controlling man. I was over it already. I didn't want to see another man hurt her. It made me feel like it was okay to be in situations or relationships where things like this were okay. I mean why wouldn't it be if I saw her going through it! Being at the age I was, was the most critical stage, because that was the time I learned and soaked up everything around me. Which led to a lot of bad repeated behaviors. From the early sexual exposure, the up and down friendships and even watching my mom in those different relationships. I was super impressionable at this time. So many things happened to me in this short period of time that played a role in the woman I became. So many of these things are battles that I am currently having while trying to break curses for my own children. The little girl in me is screaming for help. The little girl is full of anxiety and confusion. The little girl who has been dying to find the words to express all of these different feelings. Like my mom I know I deserve happiness. I deserve love.

I deserve relationships that don't come with confusion or secrets. But that is an everyday battle of constant reassuring myself. These experiences were hard to go through but now I am ready to peel the scab off and let the womb actually heal. I'm finally ready to.... Speak.